Basic Guide to
Adobe Acrobat 2017

Version 1

Table of Contents

Adobe Acrobat

Adobe Acrobat allows you to take various documents and convert them into PDF files. PDF stands for Portable Document Format and is a standard that allows a file to appear the same on any computer without needing the original software; all that is needed is a PDF viewer, such as Adobe Acrobat Reader. A document that was created in Microsoft Word can be converted into a PDF file, and then opened on an Apple computer that does not have Word, and it will look the same as the original file.

In addition to converting files into PDFs, Acrobat also allows one to do some editing. Pages can be moved. Files can be combined together. Bookmarks and links can be added for easy navigation. Though text can be edited to a point, if there will be many changes, it would be best to edit the original document and then reconvert it.

Convert to PDF

Acrobat allows several ways to convert a file to PDF. Some programs, such as Word and Excel, will have a tab on the ribbon for PDF conversion.

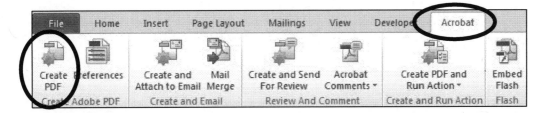

Another option is going to the File menu and seeing if there is a choice to Save As PDF.

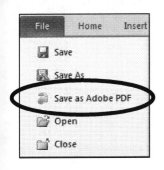   OR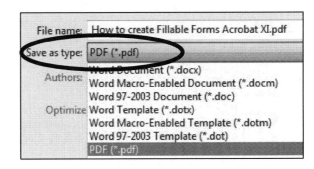

You can also go into Acrobat and choose FILE > CREATE > PDF FROM FILE.

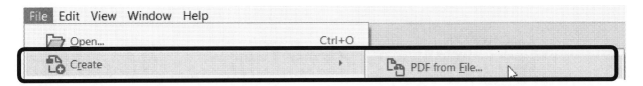

If none of the options above are available (some files cannot be converted in the ways listed above), then the final choice is to open the original document, go to FILE > PRINT, and choose Adobe PDF as the printer.

6

Work Tabs

In Acrobat Pro 2017, there are the Home, Tools, and one or more work tabs.

The Home tab gives a list of recently used files for easy access. A single click will give options to edit or export the file. Double-clicking on a file will open it.

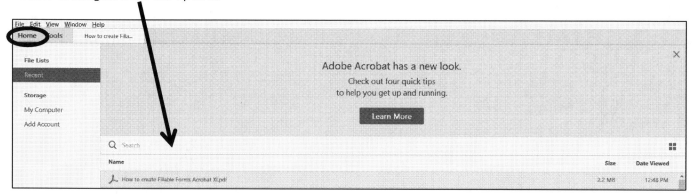

The Tools tab will have a menu of different tools available for creating and editing PDFs, as well as creating forms.

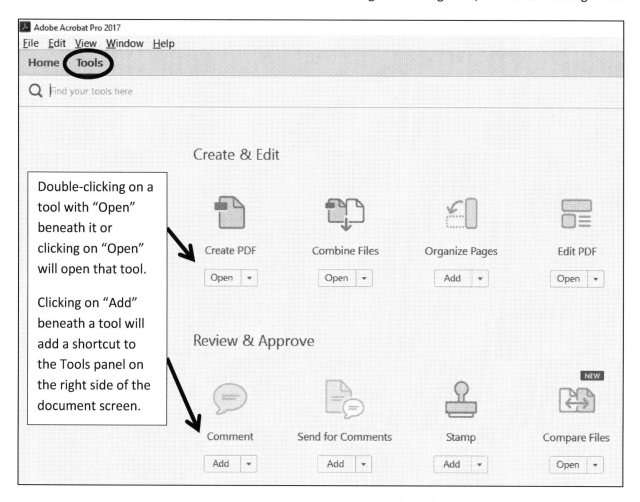

Double-clicking on a tool with "Open" beneath it or clicking on "Open" will open that tool.

Clicking on "Add" beneath a tool will add a shortcut to the Tools panel on the right side of the document screen.

As documents are opened, their names will appear in tabs just under the menu bar. The tabs can be used to switch to a file by clicking on it, or to close a file by clicking on its "x."

Thumbnails and Bookmarks

A thumbnail is a small icon of a page that allows you to jump to that page by clicking on it. A bookmark is a word or phrase that is used as a link to jump to another part of the document. Thumbnails are automatically created by Acrobat and can be displayed by clicking on the thumbnails button on the left side menu. If the left side menu is hidden, click on the arrow halfway down the left side.

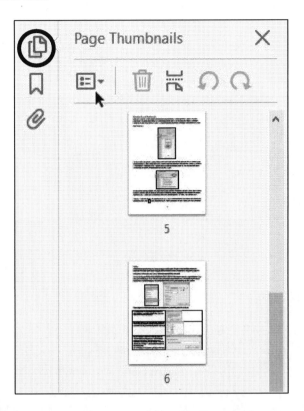

To create a bookmark, go to the page to which you wish to link the bookmark. The bookmark will remember the page's location and magnification (zoom). Click on the bookmark button on the right and choose New Bookmark. You can also go to TOOLS> EDIT PDF>MORE>ADD BOOKMARK (CTRL+B). Type in the name of the bookmark and press enter.

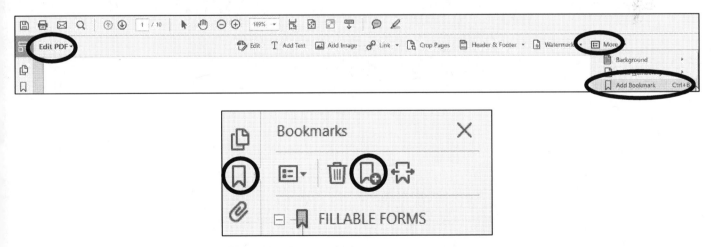

To move a bookmark up or down in the bookmark list, click and hold its icon or name and then drag it.

A bookmark can be dragged slightly to the right when being moved. This will make it a sub-bookmark (as shown with the three sub-bookmarks under the Fillable Forms bookmark in the photo below). Dragging it back to the left will make it a regular bookmark. Sub-bookmarks can be hidden or revealed by clicking on the "+/-" next to the main bookmark.

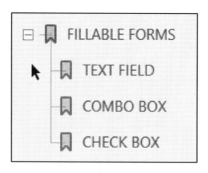

To trigger a bookmark and go to the page it represents, you need to switch to either the Selection (arrow) or Pan (hand) tool and then click on the 🔖 icon to the left of the text. Clicking on the text will open the bookmark name for editing.

Links

A link can be set up to allow a user to jump to a page or website, open a file, play a sound or video, or even run a JavaScript. Unlike the hyperlink on a web page, the PDF link is not attached to the text or an image on the page. It is attached to a box that you create. You can resize and move the link box as needed.

To make the link, go to TOOLS> EDIT PDF>LINK>ADD/EDIT WEB OR DOCUMENT LINK. Move your mouse to the page and click and drag it to create a link rectangle. A box will display asking if the link should be visible (have a border around it), if it should highlight when the link is clicked, and what action the link will execute – go to a page, file, web site, or other.

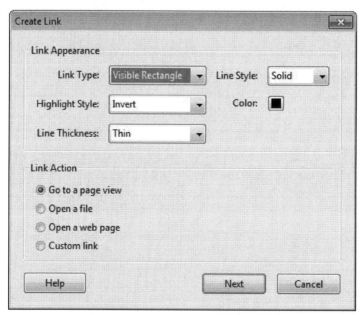

Depending on what Link Action is chosen, when you click on Next, you will get one of these boxes:

Go to a page view – scroll to the page to which you wish the link to connect. Zoom in or out as necessary. Click Set Link when you are ready.	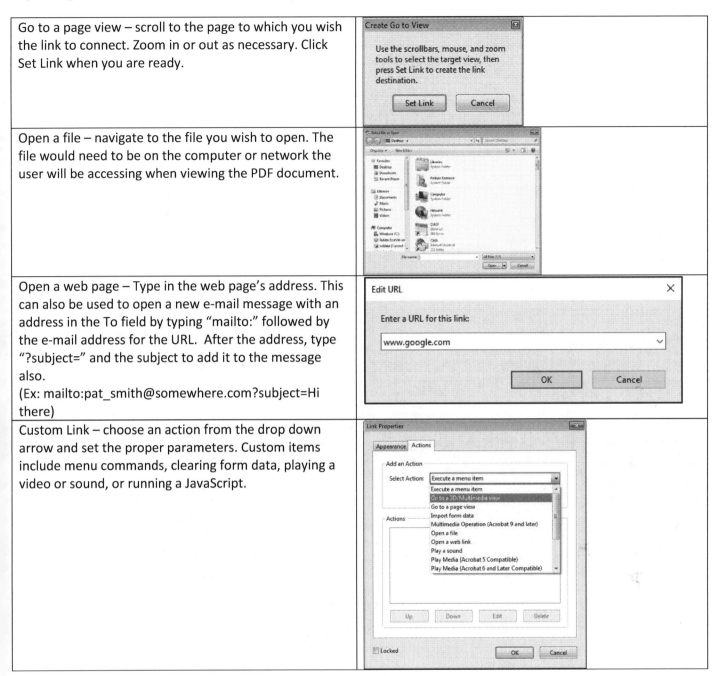
Open a file – navigate to the file you wish to open. The file would need to be on the computer or network the user will be accessing when viewing the PDF document.	
Open a web page – Type in the web page's address. This can also be used to open a new e-mail message with an address in the To field by typing "mailto:" followed by the e-mail address for the URL. After the address, type "?subject=" and the subject to add it to the message also. (Ex: mailto:pat_smith@somewhere.com?subject=Hi there)	
Custom Link – choose an action from the drop down arrow and set the proper parameters. Custom items include menu commands, clearing form data, playing a video or sound, or running a JavaScript.	

If you need to edit, resize or move the link box, make sure you are in link edit mode (TOOLS> EDIT PDF>LINK>ADD/EDIT WEB OR DOCUMENT LINK) and click on the link box. The sizing handles (squares) on the edges of the box will allow you to change the size. Just click and drag a handle. Click and hold inside the link box in order to grab it and move it to another part of the page. Double-click on the link box in order to change its action or appearance.

The link cannot be triggered while you are in edit mode. To test the link, you need to switch to either the Selection (arrow) or Pan (hand) tool.

If the link will open a file or web page, a warning will appear for the user:

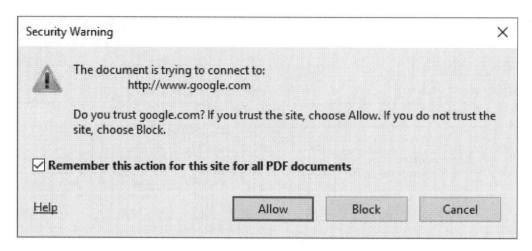

The user can then allow or block the action. If the link is to create an e-mail message, the e-mail program needs to be open.

Searching

You can search for words or phrases in a single PDF file or in all the PDF files in a folder. To do a basic search, go to EDIT>FIND. The Find box will open. Type in the word or phrase and click Next to search forward or Previous to search backwards.

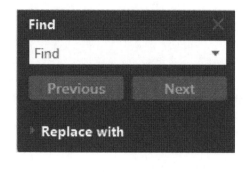

You can choose "Replace with" at the bottom of the Find box to change the word or phrase to something else.

You can also go to EDIT>ADVANCED SEARCH to get other options, such as searching bookmarks and comments or looking at all the documents in a folder.

NOTE: It will only find words if the PDF file has readable text.

Pages

Move Pages

You may need to reorder the pages in a PDF document. To do so, open the thumbnail panel on the left.

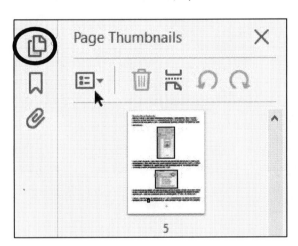

Click and drag the thumbnail of the page you wish to move above or below another page. When you see a line appear above/below the other page, release the mouse. If you need to move several pages at once, click on the first thumbnail, hold CTRL and click on the other thumbnails. When they are all selected, let go of CTRL and drag one of the thumbnails.

If you cannot drag the thumbnail, make sure the page magnification is set to fit the full page in the window.

Add Pages

Acrobat can combine PDF files together. All the pages in one will be added to the other. To add the pages of one file to another, go to TOOLS > ORGANIZE PAGES > INSERT. (You may also right-click on a thumbnail image of a page and choose Insert Pages.) Navigate to the file you wish to insert and then choose where to place the pages.

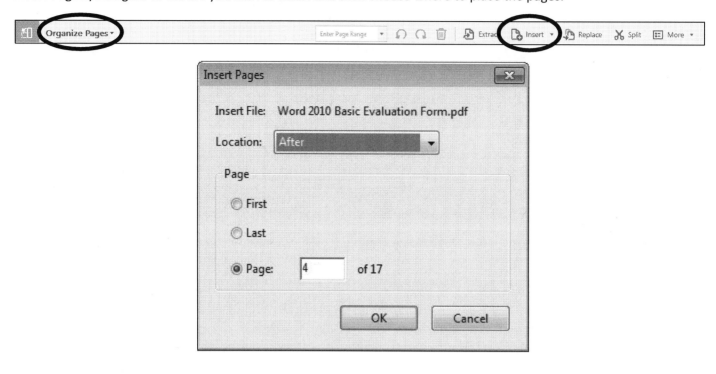

Extract Pages

If you only want some of the pages in a PDF file to be moved to another file, you can extract those pages. Go to TOOLS > ORGANIZE PAGES > EXTRACT, and select the page you wish to extract. To extract more than one page, hold the CTRL key as you click on them.

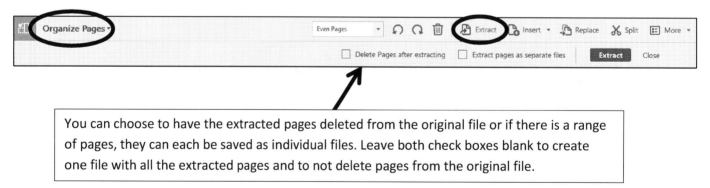

You can choose to have the extracted pages deleted from the original file or if there is a range of pages, they can each be saved as individual files. Leave both check boxes blank to create one file with all the extracted pages and to not delete pages from the original file.

Replace Pages

To swap a page or pages in a file with the page(s) in another file, go to TOOLS > ORGANIZE PAGES, and then select the page(s) you wish to replace. To select more than one page, hold the CTRL key as you click on them. Choose Replace on the toolbar and navigate to the file that has the new pages. This can also be accomplished by inserting and deleting pages, but it saves a step.

Delete Pages

To remove a page from a file, go to TOOLS > ORGANIZE PAGES, and then select the page you wish to remove. You may select the trash can on the toolbar or the one that appears on the page's thumbnail. To delete more than one page, hold the CTRL key as you click on them.

Rotate Pages

Sometimes a page needs to be shown in landscape orientation as opposed to portrait, or vice versa. In those situations, it can be rotated. To rotate the page, go to TOOLS > ORGANIZE PAGES, and then select the page you wish to rotate. You may select the rotate arrows on the toolbar or the ones that appear on the page's thumbnail. To rotate more than one page, hold the CTRL key as you click on them.

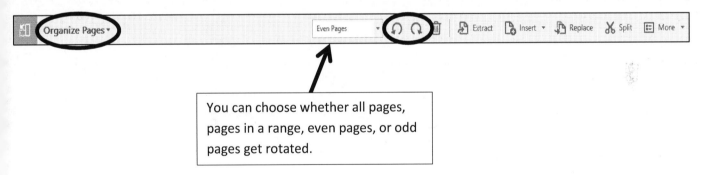

You can choose whether all pages, pages in a range, even pages, or odd pages get rotated.

Adding/Editing Text

If you need to add text to a PDF document, you can go to TOOLS> EDIT PDF >ADD TEXT. Format options will appear in the panel. Click on the page and start to type in the text box. Click and drag a border of the box to move it.

To edit text that you have typed in or that might be part of the original document, you can go to TOOLS> EDIT PDF > EDIT. Boxes will appear around all the editable text in the document. Click in a box and make your changes. Click and drag a border of the box to move it.

If the text on the page is from a scanned document, Acrobat will try to determine what is text through Optical Character Recognition. Not all documents can be converted to text and sometimes letters are translated incorrectly, such as "lo" might be translated as "b."

To exit edit text mode, close the Edit PDF toolbar or click on the Selection (arrow) or Pan (hand) tool on the toolbar.

Headers/Footers

If the original document did not have headers or footers and you wish to add them, go to TOOLS> EDIT PDF>HEADER & FOOTER. You will have choices to Add, Update, or Remove. Update will only work on headers and footers created in Acrobat. It will not affect headers and footers from the original document. Remove can remove headers and footers from the original document, as well as those created in Acrobat.

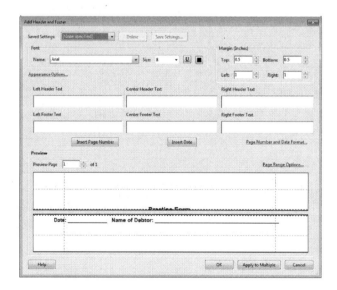

When adding a header or footer, a box will open with options for putting text in the left, center, or right side of the header/footer, adding page numbers, adding dates, and formatting items.

Watermarks

A watermark can be added as text or as a photo. To add a watermark, go to TOOLS> EDIT PDF>WATERMARK. You will have an option to Add, Update, or Remove. Update will only work on watermarks created in Acrobat. It will not affect watermarks from the original document. Remove can remove watermarks from the original document, as well as those created in Acrobat.

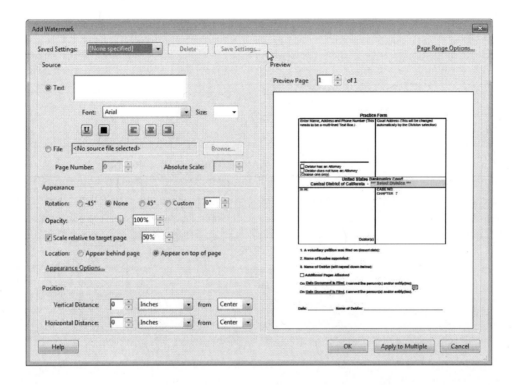

When adding, a box will open with options for using text or a file (photo). There will be choices for rotation, opacity, formatting, and placement. The Apply to Multiple button will allow the same watermark to be added to other PDF documents.

Commenting Tools

A PDF file may be passed around for comments. To access the commenting tools, click TOOLS> COMMENT.

Annotations allow you to add comment balloons, cross out text, attach files and add stamps.

Drawing Markups lets you circle items, add text boxes, add shapes, and erase markup.

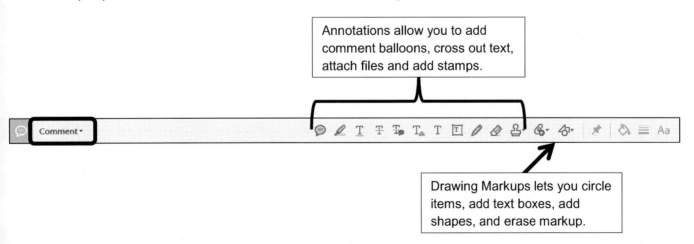

The Comment List will appear on the right. It displays all of the comments in the document.

To add the comment, choose a tool and then click and drag on the page where you wish the comment to appear. Add any text associated with the comment. You can use this method to highlight existing text in yellow or another color to point out a particular passage when making a point in a proposal. Stamps allows a choice to use a custom design. To do so, the picture to be used must be converted to a PDF file.

NOTE: Comments do not print out unless you choose Documents and Markup in the print dialog box. (See Printing)

Go to TOOLS> SEND FOR COMMENTS for options to send the document out for review and track what others are saying.

Removing Metadata

Metadata is information about the file. Whenever you create a file, the metadata is automatically created. Metadata contains information such as who is the author, when was the file created, and how many times it has been revised. Before a document is sent out, it may be desired to remove any metadata. To see the metadata in a PDF file, go to FILE > PROPERTIES. Metadata will be displayed on the Description tab with more available under ADDITIONAL METADATA. You may close the properties box when finished. To remove the metadata, go to TOOLS > REDACT > REMOVE HIDDEN INFORMATION or SANITIZE DOCUMENT.

Printing

To print a document, go to FILE > PRINT or use the Print button on the toolbar.

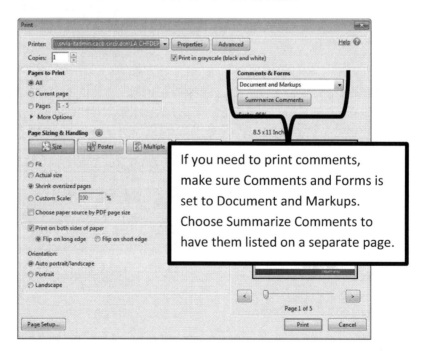

If you need to print comments, make sure Comments and Forms is set to Document and Markups. Choose Summarize Comments to have them listed on a separate page.

There will be options for how many copies, which pages to print, page orientation, and scaling.

Converting a PDF to Word

There are times when a PDF file needs to be edited in such a way that it is beyond the abilities of Acrobat. In those cases, it is best to go back to the original Word document. Unfortunately, sometimes the original document is gone and so the PDF file will need to be converted back into Word. Open the PDF file and go to TOOLS>EXPORT > MICROSOFT WORD or you can go to FILE>EXPORT TO>MICROSOFT WORD>MICROSOFT WORD.

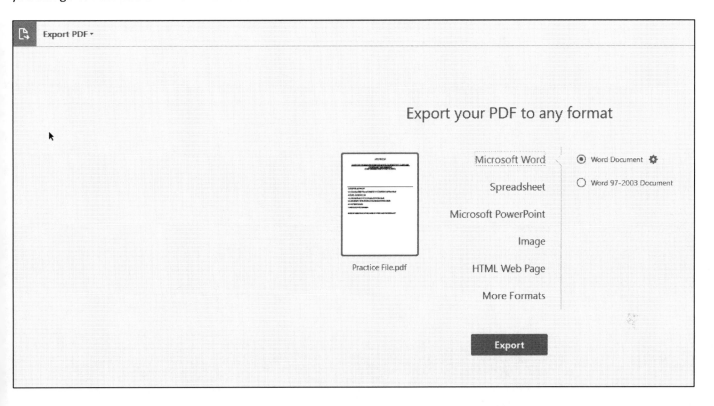

The file will take a few seconds to minutes and be converted into a Word document. Some formatting will be lost. Headers and footers will usually carry over properly, but line numbers are not understood and will become part of the page's text.

Fillable Forms

A Fillable Form in Adobe Acrobat allows a user to type in answers and then print out the form, as opposed to printing it and then filling it out by hand. This can save time and effort, avoiding such problems as illegible handwriting. Acrobat will allow a user to open the form in Acrobat Reader, fill it in and then print it. The data can be saved in the form if it is saved properly (see Saving Form Data).

It would be easiest to create the form first in Word and convert it to a PDF file. Then, open the PDF file in Acrobat and select TOOLS > PREPARE FORM.

Choose the file to make into a form. And click on "Start." If form field auto detection is on, then Acrobat will automatically create the form fields in the file. If you do not want it to automatically create fields, then click "Change."

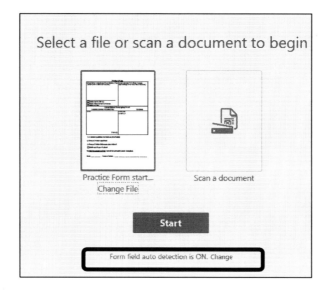

If you chose "Change" in the previous step, then this box will appear.

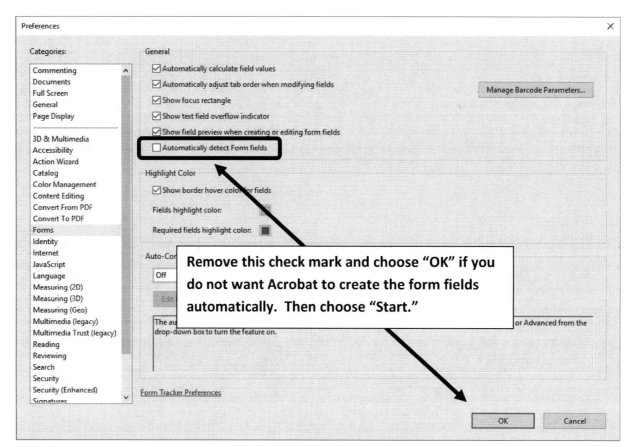

Remove this check mark and choose "OK" if you do not want Acrobat to create the form fields automatically. Then choose "Start."

You can choose a form tool from the toolbar.

Text Field

The most common type of form control used is the Text Field. It allows the user to fill in names, dates, numbers or several lines of information. The Text Field can be formatted so only certain types of data are accepted.

On the Forms Toolbar, or in the "Add New Field" list, select the Text Field button. Placement guides will assist in positioning the field. Click on the page where the form field should appear.

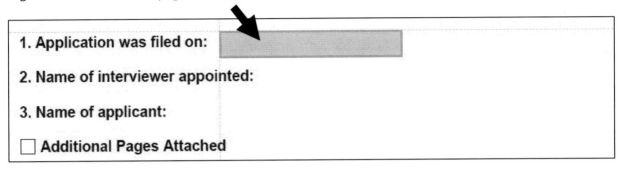

The Field Properties Dialog box will display.

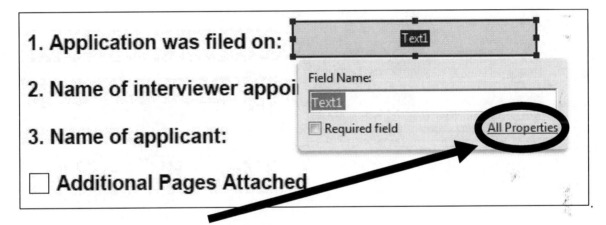

Click on "All Properties" to open the Text Field Properties box.

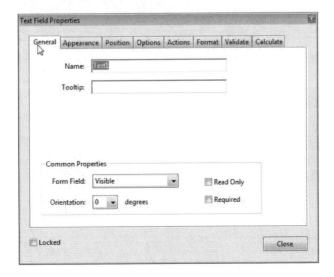

When utilizing a Text Field there are several properties that can be adjusted. The field can be resized and repositioned after the properties box is closed. Most of the following properties are the same for all fields.

General properties allow you to Name the field or use a default name such as Text1, add pop-up Tooltip text, and declare whether the field is visible or can print, is Read Only and cannot be changed, is Required, or is at an angle. The Locked option will prevent the field from being moved on the page during editing.

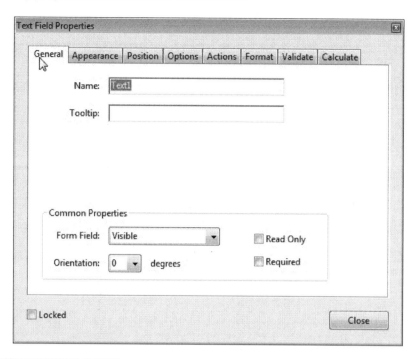

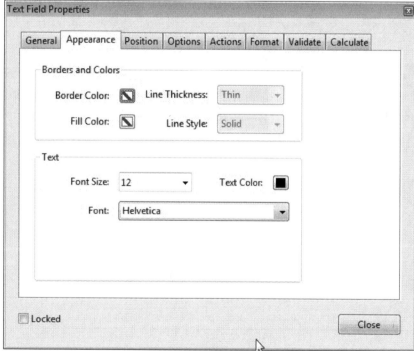

Appearance properties allow you to choose if the Text Field will have a border, the color and style of the border and the inside fill of the box, the Font Size (Auto will re-adjust the text to the size of the box), and the Font type and color.

Position properties allow you to set the location of the field on the page by using measurements instead of adjusting the placement manually.

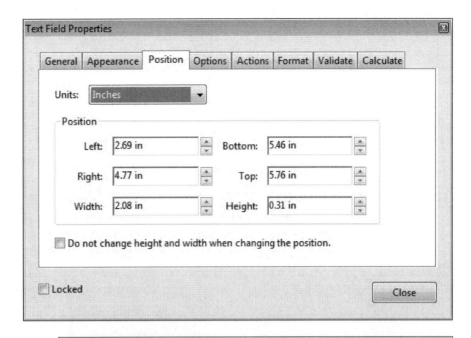

Options properties deal with changing the Alignment of text in the box, what text is already in the box, whether the box can hold a single or multiple line response, if formatting is allowed, how many characters can be typed and if spelling should be checked. Users can also make the field hide passwords, add a file path and spread out the spacing or comb of the characters.

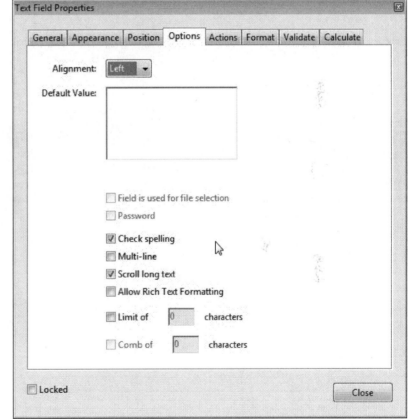

Actions allow some event to occur that the field triggers (such as the file is saved or another field is filled-in also). The triggers are might be caused by the mouse (Mouse Up, Mouse Down) or by interacting with the field while using the Tab key or other option (On Focus, On Blur). Actions can be selected from a list or a JavaScript can be created.

Format can be used to limit what type of data is entered into the Text Field:

- Number
- Percentage
- Date
- Time
- Special
- Custom

Each selection will have its own options.

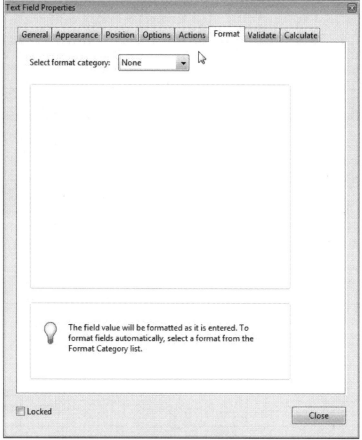

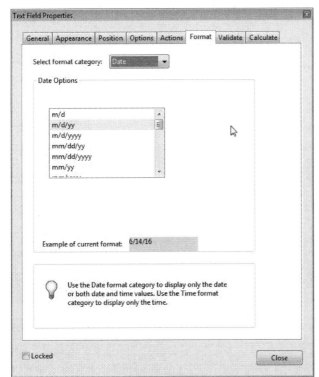

Date Format

Number Format

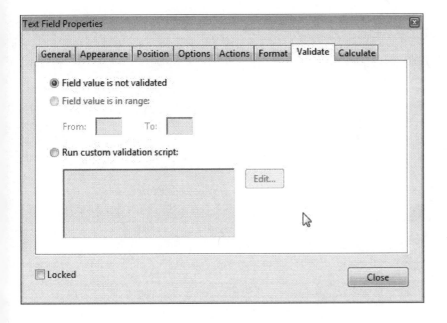

Validate can ensure a number entered falls within a certain range, or a JavaScript can be created to verify a custom rule (such as ensuring an email address is entered properly).

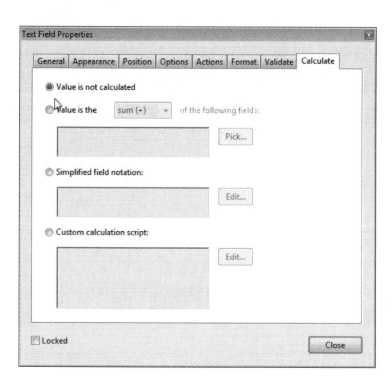

Calculate is used to automatically fill in a field based on numbers or data added to other fields. Basic mathematical functions and JavaScript can be used.

There is a Calendar Field on the toolbar that will place a Text Field with the Format option set to Date.

Drop-Down Box

The Drop-Down Menu, also known as a Combo Box, allows the form to limit the answers a user may enter by giving them a selection list. To add a drop-down menu, click on the Drop-Down Menu button on the Forms Toolbar.

Placement guides will assist in positioning the field. Click on the page where the form field should appear.

The Drop-Down Menu Properties Dialog box will display.

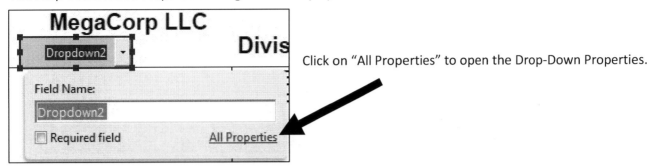

Click on "All Properties" to open the Drop-Down Properties.

When utilizing a Drop-Down there are several properties that can be adjusted. The properties are the same as the Text Field, with the exception of the Options tab. The field can be resized and repositioned after the properties box is closed.

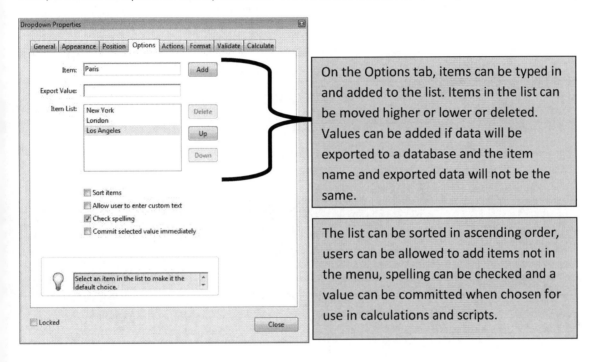

On the Options tab, items can be typed in and added to the list. Items in the list can be moved higher or lower or deleted. Values can be added if data will be exported to a database and the item name and exported data will not be the same.

The list can be sorted in ascending order, users can be allowed to add items not in the menu, spelling can be checked and a value can be committed when chosen for use in calculations and scripts.

Check Box

The Check Box tool allows the user to choose one or more items by clicking in a small square. The Check Box allows for "Yes/No" answers through a visual graphic.

Placement guides will assist in positioning the field. Click on the page where the form field should appear.

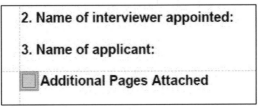

2. Name of interviewer appointed:

3. Name of applicant:

☐ **Additional Pages Attached**

The Check Box Properties Dialog box will display.

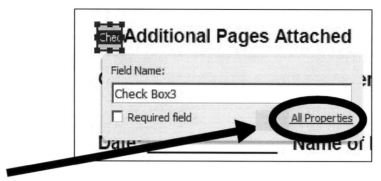

Click on "All Properties" to open the Check Box Properties.

When utilizing a Check Box, there are several properties that can be adjusted. The properties are the same as for the Text Field, with the exceptions of the Options tab and the missing Validation and Calculation tabs. The field can be resized and repositioned after the properties box is closed.

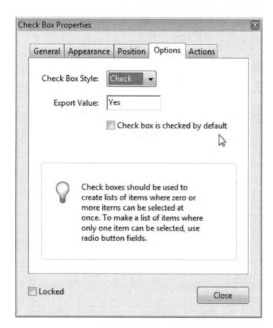

On the Options tab, a style for the appearance of the check mark can be chosen:

- Check
- Circle
- Cross (X)
- Diamond
- Square
- Star

A value can be added if data is to be exported to a database and the box can be checked automatically before the form is filled in.

Radio Buttons

Radio Buttons are used when only one choice out of two or more options is allowed. All options are seen and only one is chosen. If another is chosen, the previous option is deselected.

To add Radio Buttons, click on the button on the Forms Toolbar. Placement guides will assist in positioning the field. Click on the page where the form field should appear.

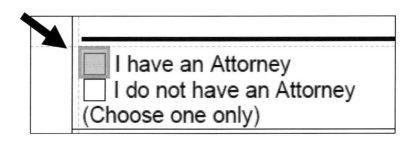

The Radio Buttons Properties Dialog will display. The Radio Buttons properties have two name fields. The Choice field is different for each button. The Group field needs to be the same for all related Radio Buttons. An example would be a "Choose your Gender:" question. The Radio Button Choice for the first button might be "Male" and the Radio Button Choice for the second button might be "Female." However, the Group name for both buttons would be "Gender" so Acrobat knows the buttons are related or grouped together.

Click on "All Properties" to open the Combo Box Properties.

To add another button, click on "Add another button" or use EDIT>COPY and then EDIT>PASTE.

When utilizing Radio Buttons, there are several properties that can be adjusted. The properties are the same as for the Text Field, with the exceptions of the Options tab and the missing Validation and Calculation tabs. The field can be resized and repositioned after the properties box is closed. In order to have the Radio Buttons work together in a group, the Name (General Tab) of each must be the same and the Export Value (Options Tab) must be different. The Export Values can be anything: Yes/No, True/False, A/B/C/D, 1/2/3, etc.

A style for the appearance of the Radio Button can be chosen on the Options tab:

- Check
- Circle
- Cross
- Diamond
- Square
- Star

A button can be checked automatically before the form is filled in and multiple buttons can be chosen at once if the name and value are the same.

Button

The Button tool is used to either submit or clear a form or run an action (see the Action Tab section).

To add a Button, click on the Button on the Forms Toolbar. Placement guides will assist in positioning the field. Click on the page where the form field should appear.

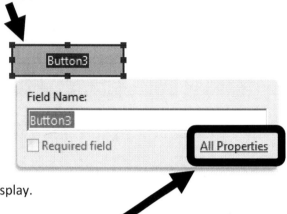

The Button Properties dialog will display.

Click on "All Properties" to open the Button Properties.

When utilizing a Button, there are several properties that can be adjusted. The properties are the same as for the Text Field, with the exceptions of the Options tab and the missing Validation and Calculation tabs. The field can be resized and repositioned after the properties box is closed.

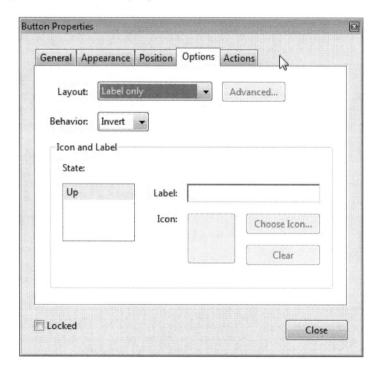

On the Options tab, the Layout can be changed for how the button displays with a label and/or an icon.

The Behavior determines how the button appears when clicked.

The State allows you to change the text and icon (image) when the button is up, down, or rolled over. The Behavior must be set to Push to change more than the Up state.

Actions Tab

The Action Tab is standard to all the form fields, though it is mostly used for the Button field. It allows the designer to add some interactivity beyond just filling in fields. An action is triggered when a field is either selected or de-selected.

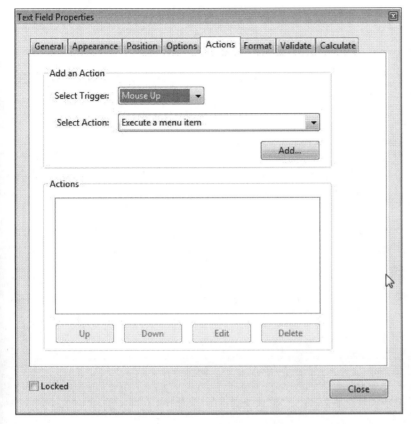

The triggers for an action are:

- Mouse Up – someone has clicked on the field and released the mouse.
- Mouse Down – Someone has clicked on a field and has not released the mouse.
- Mouse Enter – the mouse has moved into/over the field.
- Mouse Exit – the mouse has moved away from the field.
- On Focus – a field is selected by either using the mouse or the tab key.
- On Blur – a field is no longer selected.

After choosing a trigger, an action is then selected from the Select Action dropdown list. Most of the actions are pretty self-explanatory. If an action is being attached to a Button, the usual choices are Submit a Form or Reset a Form. After the action is selected, click on "Add." A new box will open requesting more information, such as to what web address will the form information be submitted, which fields get reset, what menu item is triggered, or what is the JavaScript that must be run. To edit an action, click on the action, not the trigger, in the list of actions and choose "Edit" or "Delete." If an action does not run, it could be that you need to choose a different trigger.

JavaScript

JavaScript is a scripting language used to enhance a program or a web page. There are certain syntaxes and rules one must follow. JavaScript can be added to the document, a page, or any form field, thereby automating certain aspects of the file. An example would be that the user can make a selection from a Dropdown Box and instantly another field is populated with information. Or, if a field is left blank, the script can alert the user to the missing data.

Here is a sample script that will change the color of the text in a Dropdown Box named "division" to red if the default value of "*** Select Division ***" is displayed, and will turn the text to black if any other choice is made:

```
var originaltext="*** Select Division ***";
var choice=this.getField("division");
if (choice.value==originaltext) {
choice.textColor=new Array("RGB",255,0,0);
} else {
choice.textColor = new Array("G",0);
}
```

The term **var** creates a variable, which holds text or a number for later use. The text ***this.getField("division")*** tells the script to look for a field with the name **division** in the document. An ***If…Then…Else*** statement is created to see if the variable of **choice** is equal to the variable of **originaltext**. Then, if the values are equal, the color of the text is changed to red (**RGB** is Red, Green, Blue). If the values are not equal, the color of the text is changed to black (**G** is for a shade of Gray). **Array** tells the script that the value being added to the variable has more than one possibilty. JavaScript is case-sensitive; whereas **textColor** is understood in the script, **textcolor** or **Textcolor** would cause an error.

When adding an action to a field, there is a choice to "Run a JavaScript." A small dialog box is launched to accept the JavaScript. If the script has a syntax error in it, the box will not close when "OK" is chosen. A line number that tells where an error occurs will be given, but it will not tell you what is wrong.

JavaScript is a language that must be learned and Adobe has its own "dialect" to work with their products. Information can be found in communities online.

Tab Order

When a user fills in a form, they may use their Tab key instead of their mouse to move from one field to the next. The order that the fields are selected is known as the Tab Order and it is determined by the order that the fields were added to the document.

If the Tab Order of the fields needs to be changed, go to Fields and choose the Tab Order menu. You can select "Order Tabs Manually" and then move them in the list or "Order Tabs by Row," which will order them from the top of the page to the bottom.

In the sample below, the "Order Tabs by Row" would set the Tab Order as follows: name, attorney, Group4, division. The "Order Tabs by Column" would set the Tab Order as follows: name, Group4, division, attorney.

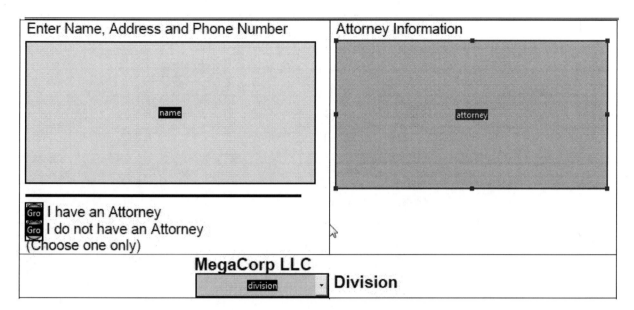

Digital Signatures

The Digital Signature tool allows a user to add their digital signature to a document, ensuring that they were the last one to make changes. On the Forms Toolbar, select the Digital Signature button.

Placement guides will assist in positioning the field. Click on the page where the form field should appear.

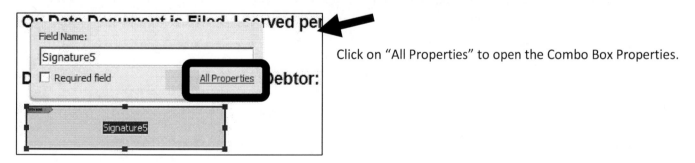

Click on "All Properties" to open the Combo Box Properties.

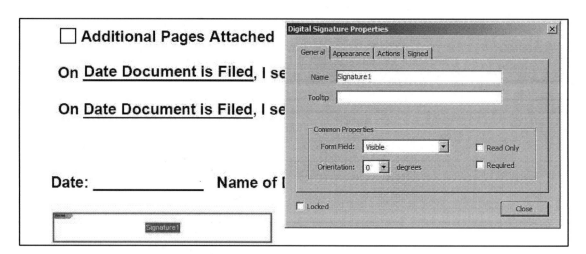

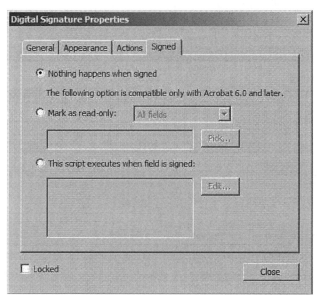

When utilizing a Digital Signature, there are several properties that can be adjusted. The properties are the same as for the Text Field, with the exceptions of the missing Options, Validation and Calculation tabs, and the addition of the Signed tab. The Signed tab allows fields to become read-only or a script to be run when the document is signed. The field can be resized and repositioned after the properties box is closed. Signing automatically saves the document. If changes are made to a document after it is signed, the signature is no longer valid.

Saving Form Data

Users may want to save the data they have typed into a form and print it out later or email it. If they are using Adobe Acrobat Reader, this is not possible, unless Reader's features are extended. Go to FILE > SAVE AS OTHER > READER EXTENDED PDF > ENABLE MORE TOOLS.

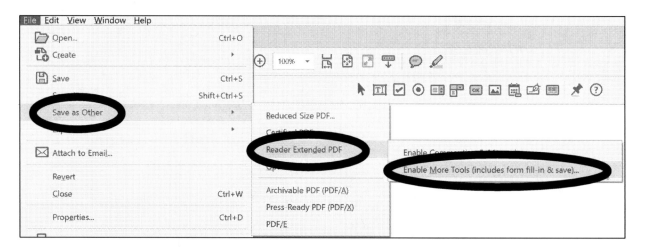

A dialog box will open, explaining what will function in Acrobat Reader. It will also save the file. (The file may be given a different name or location.)

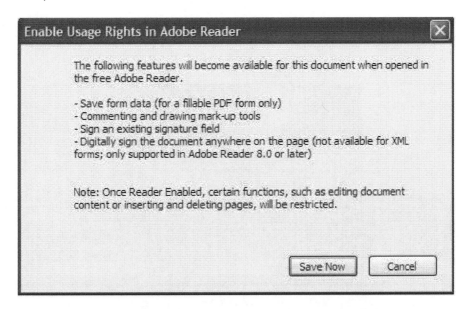

Once features are extended, the form cannot be edited directly in Acrobat Professional. A copy can be made and edited.

Clear Form Data

While editing the form, if you need to clear any data added to the form fields, go to the side panel and choose MORE > CLEAR FORM.

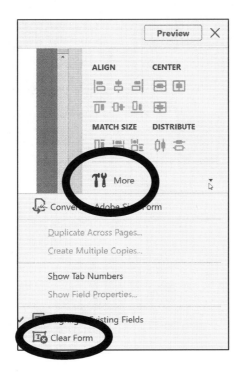

Password Security

When a document is completed, but before it is released to others, it should be password protected so changes to the overall document cannot be made. Users with Adobe Acrobat Reader will only be able to fill in the form fields, but users with Adobe Acrobat Professional would be able to change anything they wanted if password protection was not applied. To enforce security on the document, go to FILE>PROPERTIES.

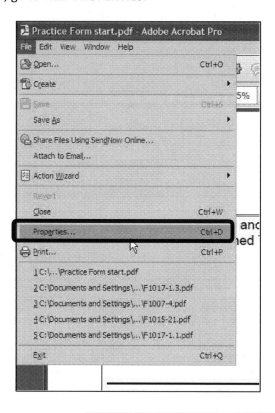

The Document Properties box will appear. Go to Security tab and click on the dropdown arrow by Security Method. Change the selection from "No Security" to "Password Security." The Password Security Settings box will appear.

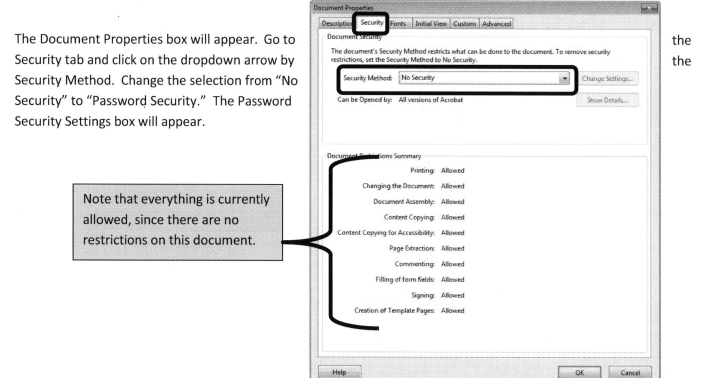

Note that everything is currently allowed, since there are no restrictions on this document.

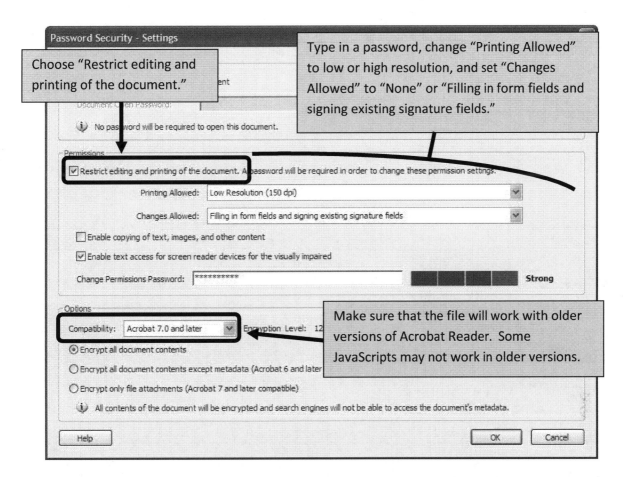

Choose "Restrict editing and printing of the document."

Type in a password, change "Printing Allowed" to low or high resolution, and set "Changes Allowed" to "None" or "Filling in form fields and signing existing signature fields."

Make sure that the file will work with older versions of Acrobat Reader. Some JavaScripts may not work in older versions.

After the changes are made, click on the "OK" button. A dialogue box may appear regarding the fact that 3rd party software might ignore the security settings. Another dialogue box will appear asking to confirm the password. Re-type the password used to restrict editing to continue. A third dialogue box will explain that the security changes will not go into effect until after the file has been saved. Save the file and the password will be applied. To remove or change the security, just return to the Document Properties Security tab and change the Security Method to "No Security" or click on the "Change Settings" button.

The additional security options are certificate security which would need digital certificates to be created and Adobe LiveCycle Rights Management which is a subscription based account from Adobe.

Made in the USA
Coppell, TX
04 November 2020